Letters

From

Gardenia

Your soul may rest in Heaven.

# Letters From Gardenia

Denae Terese Hintze

*poems*

I hope after my time has passed,
I still exist somewhere
beneath the trees,
watching as our story continues
to unfold, long after
my time here has passed

I will paint myself a picture
with the words that I write,
My searching soul knows
there are emotions to define
Bound by inarticulate nature
behind a corporeal structure,
my presence here is
looking to realign

If I can just gather the
courage to bring together
the pieces inside my mind,
painting will become easier
with every day new
emotions to define

*Denae Terese Hintze*

I believe there is a world beyond our defaults, and I will spend my life trying to become how it makes me feel

Do you think some minds are
made for a distant future that
may never be seen in our lifetime?
That it is possible to expand
larger than the sky,
and walk these lonesome streets
always wondering why..

Why do we do the things we do,
and why do we live like
we will always have tomorrow?

*Denae Terese Hintze*

There are nearly 8 billion
people in this world,
yet oftentimes I find myself
alone in a single room

Nearly 8 billion
people in this world,
and no one knows
how to use their words
with one another

8 billion
and somehow this room
feels more whole to myself
than one full of people
never using more words
than their hands can count

I want to know you beyond
the defaults you build
in front of your world,

There has to be more than
what my eyes are meeting

Because when I gazed into my own,
I found a whole other world
I had come to know

# Letters From Gardenia

Home is the space within
you wherever you go
If you look at it this way,
no matter
what changes happen
you will always have home
No one can ever take
it from you
if you make
your heart a home

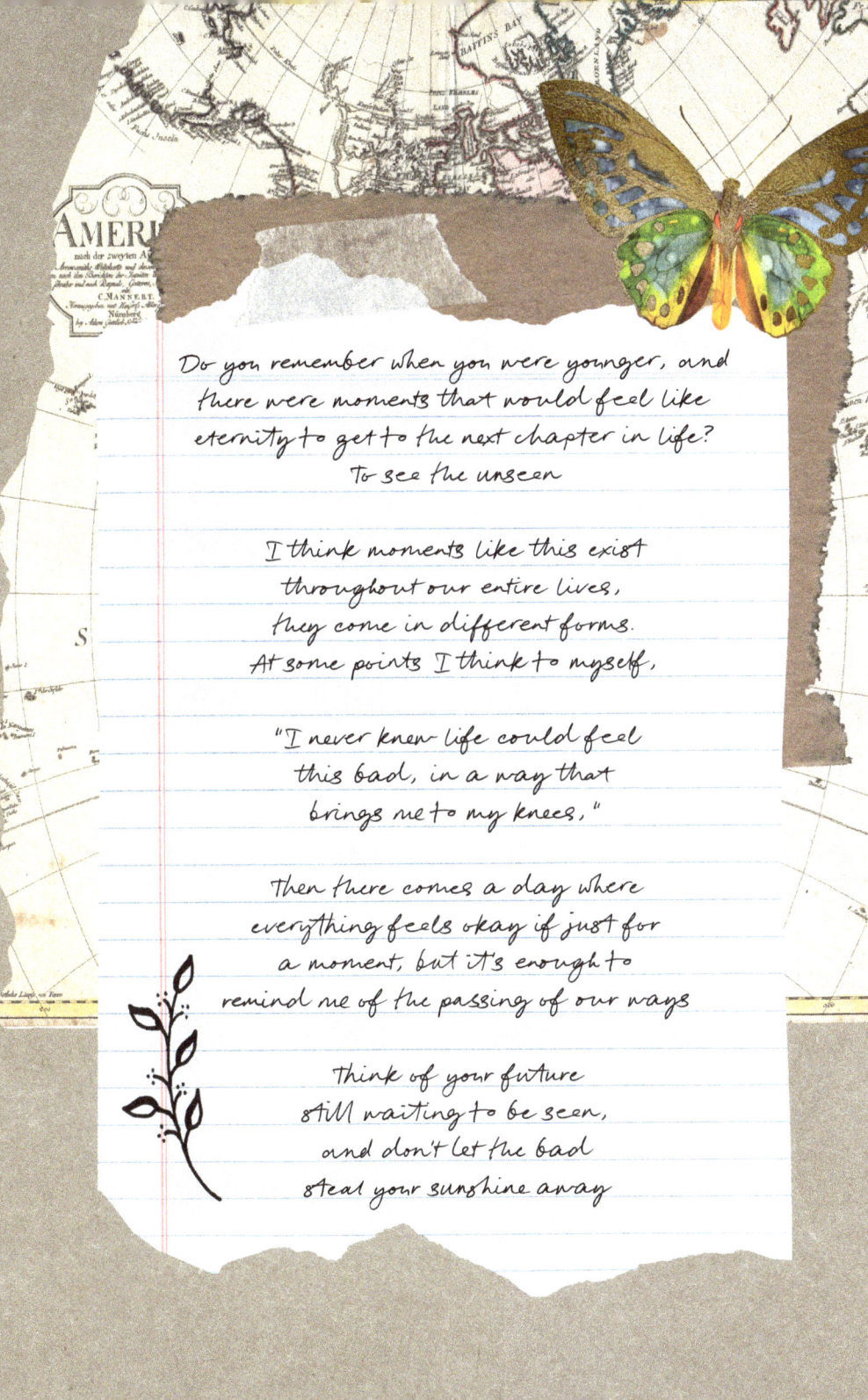

Do you remember when you were younger, and there were moments that would feel like eternity to get to the next chapter in life?
To see the unseen

I think moments like this exist throughout our entire lives, they come in different forms. At some points I think to myself,

"I never knew life could feel this bad, in a way that brings me to my knees,"

Then there comes a day where everything feels okay if just for a moment, but it's enough to remind me of the passing of our ways

Think of your future still waiting to be seen, and don't let the bad steal your sunshine away

# Time

A song that sings
to us in silence,
The invisible fabric
of our lives
Our past unfolding
into the future,
Every life
is on the line

Timing feels
different for everyone,
Not just as the
hands tick on by
Some seconds
are sung in sighs,
while others
sing hymns of our soul
Moments forever
sealed within our bones

People come and go,
but there are some
I think I will love
silently for the
rest of my life

If there was a song about silence,
It would whisper a gentle tune

Filled in the empty stardust
dancing between me and you

LIKE A ROADMAP TO THIS WORLD, I WILL TRACE THE MAP OF MY HEART DOWN TO THE ROOT OF MY SOUL

Some might say a thought does not exist unless it is written down, a valid proof that articulates to others what it is you are trying to express. I am familiar with the yearning to be understood, but I also believe in the unspoken just as much. I believe there are feelings left undescribed and they breathe all around us, an inarticulate language of emotion that is just as valuable.

*Denae Terese Hintze*

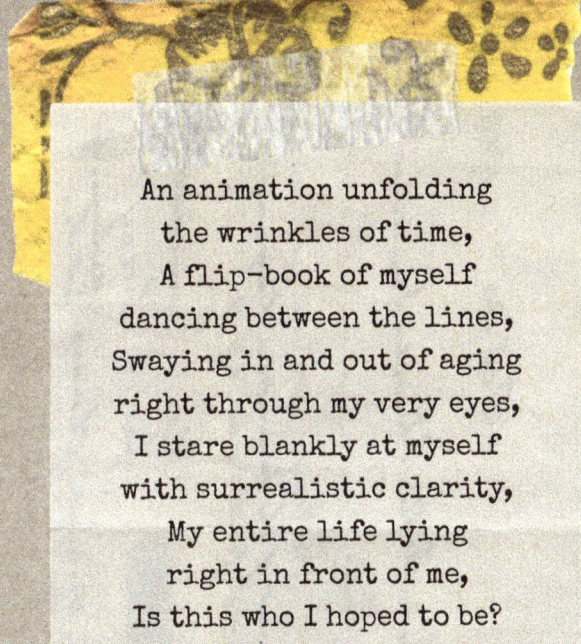

An animation unfolding
the wrinkles of time,
A flip-book of myself
dancing between the lines,
Swaying in and out of aging
right through my very eyes,
I stare blankly at myself
with surrealistic clarity,
My entire life lying
right in front of me,
Is this who I hoped to be?

**Denae Terese Hintze**

Some people hold so much inside of them,
they build a strong wall around them
A facade of perfection

I NOW PRACTICE FACING DIFFICULT EMOTIONS RATHER THAN ESCAPING THEM
IT IS CLEAR TO ME NO MATTER HOW MUCH I PREOCCUPY MYSELF,
THEY WILL ALWAYS BE IN THE SHADOWS WAITING TO FIND MEANING IN MY RELEASE

Addiction to anything
can be the most
dangerous force.
Your body is tricked
into believing the only way
to feel is more

Addiction causes you
to lose sight of
your own resilience,
Making you believe
you need it to prove
you are confident

If you let go of addiction,
you are able to gain
a forgotten clarity
Once hidden behind
a dysfunctional capacity,
Revealed by a sense of familiarity
the moment you start
to heal from uncertainty

## Somewhere in the Middle of the Day

I was present, but also distant in my frame of mind. In between black outs and soaring thoughts, it took everything I had to hold on to the smallest bit of myself. My essence carried on while there was an imbalance in my intellect. My perception was long shattered by the aches hidden behind the walls I had built around my heart. The ironic part of it all was finding those aches to be the very things that came to surface in my moments of despair. This pain I hid seemed far from pain after all when I found myself deeper than even the darkest parts of myself, holding on to them as a means of survival. Those were the things that helped me remember who I was. It was then I realized that just because things don't always go as we hoped, or people don't always fill the spaces in our lives the way we imagined, doesn't make them or life any less valuable. It just means they were meant to exist to help shape us. They were meant to exist to help us find ourselves.

# i stray into the night

> forgetting everything
> I thought I found
> I am twirling with
> no destination in sight,
> A black swan under distress,
> lost at a war of mindlessness

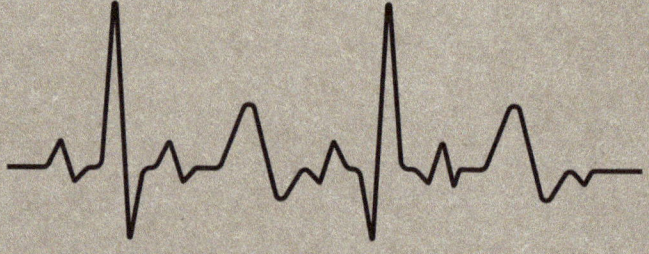

A man in uniform
walked up to me and asked
what I was looking for

We were at a park somewhere in Wisconsin,
and I remember staring blankly across
the park field, there were children playing

I turned to him and told him
how I wanted to save the children

He asked me if I knew where I was,
I did but lost sight of my car
What felt like a moment of arrestment,
turned into a moment of him rescuing me
We found my car just into town
He let me go so that I could drown

## 48 Hours

Blinded by my internal fight
I was on the brink of something more,
or was it neurotoxicity?
12, 20, 32 hours into my crusade,
Driving around aimlessly,
I remember a moment so vividly

I can almost see myself there,
Being back in my car,
looking up at the final sunrise
on some country backroad,

Angry at my existence,
I had it up to here
with my confusion,
Stepping on the gas,
feeling my hands
let go of the wheel

I closed my eyes screaming
Thinking I could escape how I feel,
Seconds perceived as minutes
until I peeled my eyes open,
My vision blended into animation
I swore I was speeding through stoplights,
but all I can truly remember is
that my heart was beating
I will never know what really happened
Just a fragmentation of memory,
The only thing I can grasp
is that it wasn't time for me

There is something about being deprived of your element that reveals a new outlook on life

At first it's uncomfortable, almost unbearable, but often times it turns out to be pivotal

## The Other Side of Mental Illness

Is what happens on the
inside while everyone else
catches only a glimpse of it,
Physically healthy with
a storm at your inner core,
A disconnect of the intellect

Others might treat you like
you aren't even there,
While thoughts are racing
and all you can do is stare

This momentary mindlessness
weaves in and out of consciousness,
Reality trying to fit a mold,
but the only belief in existence
is your own hand to hold

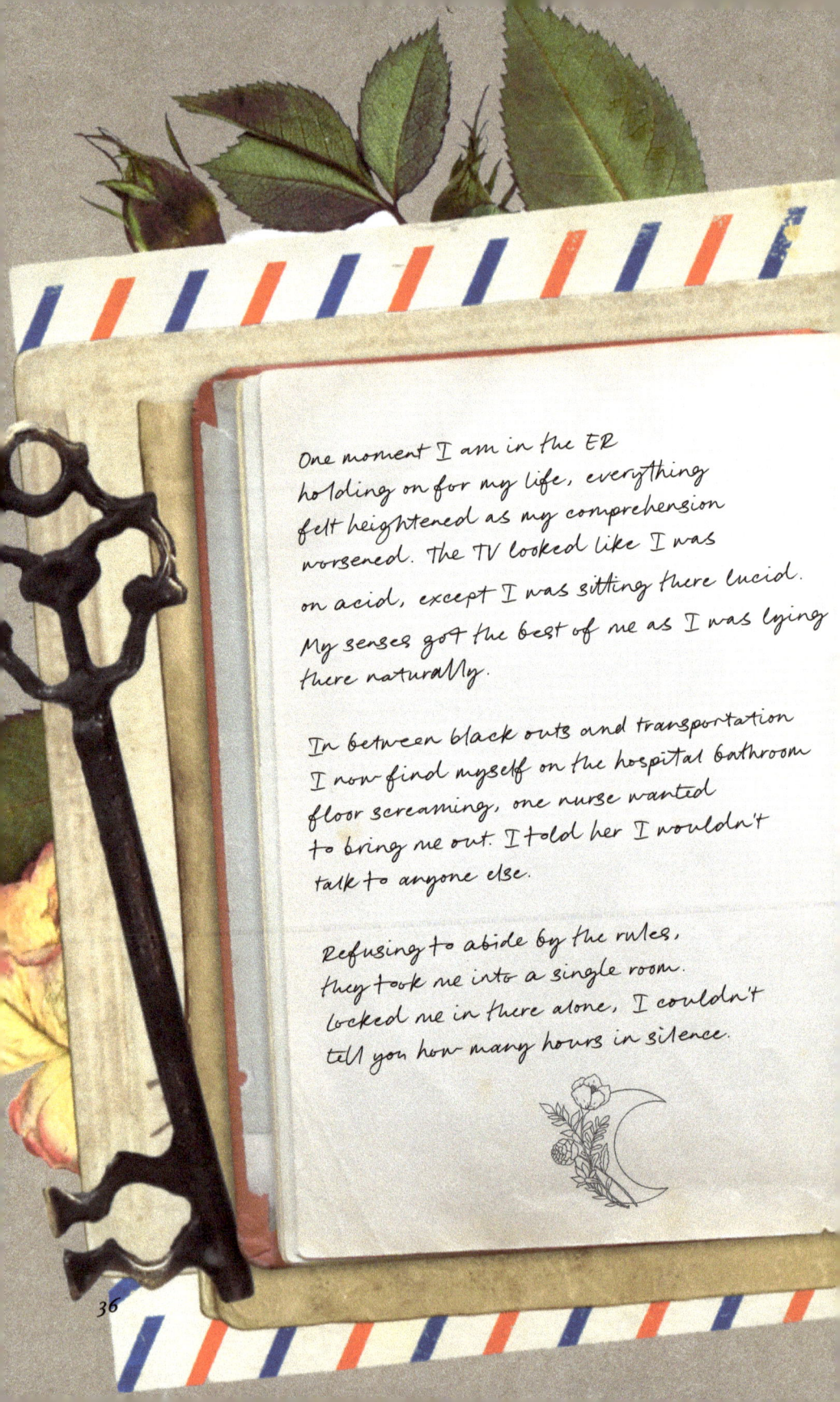

One moment I am in the ER holding on for my life, everything felt heightened as my comprehension worsened. The TV looked like I was on acid, except I was sitting there lucid. My senses got the best of me as I was lying there naturally.

In between black outs and transportation I now find myself on the hospital bathroom floor screaming, one nurse wanted to bring me out. I told her I wouldn't talk to anyone else.

Refusing to abide by the rules, they took me into a single room. Locked me in there alone, I couldn't tell you how many hours in silence.

My psyche had only gotten worse with time
before they took further steps to put me in line.
Held me down as I screamed even louder,
shot me in each arm with tranquilizers.

I fell to the ground crying in pain,
crawled to the connecting bathroom
fighting the weight.
Drowsiness took over within moments of time,
I let go as if my life was no longer mine.

My next memory is waking up in bed,
unsure of how much time had passed,
with a roommate next to me whom I never met.

Language felt unfamiliar to me,
numbness reached another level in me.
I sat there unable to form words,
I felt like an inarticulate harboring
the trauma I had just endured.

DEEP DOWN I KNEW THINGS
WOULD NEVER BE THE SAME,
EVEN THOUGH I WAS FORCED
TO GO BACK TO OLD WAYS

DAYS TURNED INTO WEEKS,
INTO MONTHS FROM MY DARK PHASE

LIFE WENT ON LIKE
IT NEVER HAPPENED,
BUT I STILL HELD
ON TO IT WONDERING WHY

When you are somewhere
in between life and death,
and you're no longer sure
if you can put up a fight,
Just remember if your
heart is still beating,
Your story isn't over yet
There is more you haven't
found light in yet

It has been six years of healing,
trying to wrap my brain
around what happened to me
Learning to trust my mind again,
Failing to realign with society
I feel like I'm on
the outside looking in,
Somewhere between where we are
and into the unknown

My survival tactics got the best of me
Past delusions still have a hold of me
Part of me tells me to let go
of what I once thought I believed,
While the other is giving them
too much meaning,
As if the Universe had
a message I was receiving,
I am somewhere in between
of what is and what is meant to be

To be selfless means to
unlearn all that surrounds you,
find yourself at the
emptiness of your core
and remain beating

*Denae Terese Hintze*

There is a truth beyond the eye can see,
and louder than the mind can speak

I AM HERE TO REMIND MYSELF THIS HEART NOT ONLY BEATS FOR ME,

BUT FOR THE TRUTH OF THE UNSEEN IN THIS WORLD OF MAKE-BELIEVE

SHE IS TIMELESS

NOT HOW SHE LOOKS,

BUT FOR THE WAY

SHE SEES BEYOND THE VEILS

OF OUR REALITY

Denae Terese Hintze

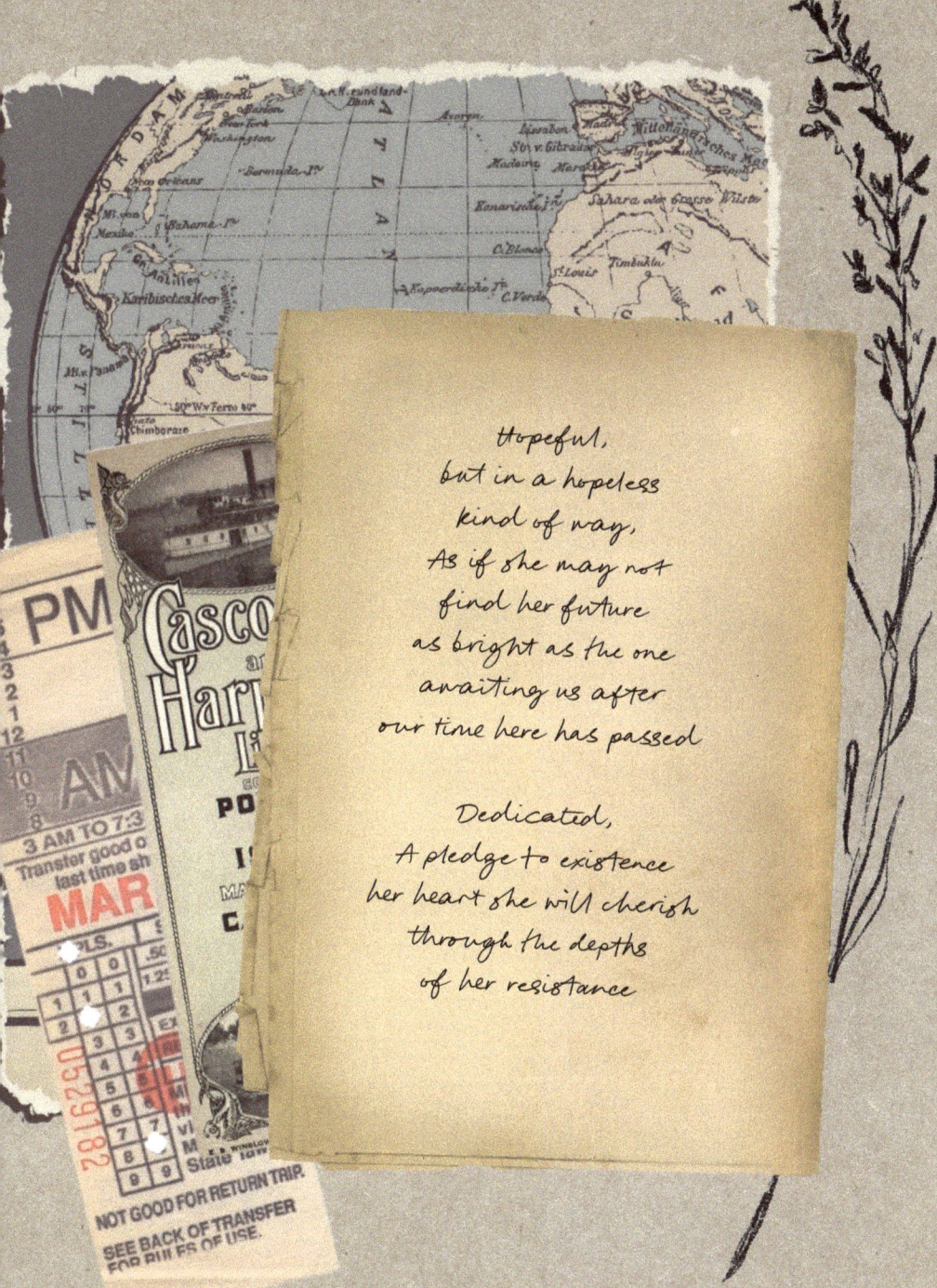

Hopeful,
but in a hopeless
kind of way,
As if she may not
find her future
as bright as the one
awaiting us after
our time here has passed

Dedicated,
A pledge to existence
her heart she will cherish
through the depths
of her resistance

*Letters From Gardenia*

I'll take Interstellar
into my deranged thoughts
and place Cooper
in the fifth dimension

Connect ideas of after-life
to morse code in
Murphy's bedroom

Psychics and mediums
believe in signs,
but are considered liars
to a blind eye

After-all,
not all signs are signs
Sometimes they are
just our interpretation
of life between dimensions

There is a thin line between the
comprehensible and incomprehensible,
sparks of indirection trying
to fit a mold,
taking shape absorbing
into a single world,
every thought drawing
from our minds appeal,
how do we decide which one is real?

We were born into a paved out world,
but that doesn't mean every
unfamiliar thought is wrong,
I believe it has to do
with finding our way
through survival
and disorder,
allowing space to find
what it means to be mortal

I am standing in the middle of a road, under
a dark, night sky looking for direction
from memory absorbing into a different perspective

Swaying between what is real and a life
that is hardly in my possession.
Just a ghost of me, escaping who I used to be

WHAT ONCE WAS ALL,

UNTIL WONDER

WHISPERED TO ME

WITH EVERY NIGHTFALL

I once had a dream a time traveler
  interrupted the present
and came to visit me.
   He looked rugged,
like he had been through a lot.
   I asked him how he got here,
he told me he and his boss
ran into a tree.

I stared blankly for a moment,
  and as I decided to get him some water
I couldn't help but think,

  Is this where death leads?

Sometimes I wonder what life would be like if we all hadn't been brought up the way we have. Where we were conditioned to believe this is everything we must be doing.

Sometimes I wonder what life would be like if all the things we must do in order to survive lived quietly in the background, allowing us to live the lives we truly wanted to live

Sometimes I wonder if the beauty that goes left unsaid carries on even long after we are gone

This imperfect gift of life
keeps me warm but dry,
An abundance of energy
filling the spaces of
a conditioned reality

What will it take to
turn this around for me?
To pull away from this
narrow line of mortality

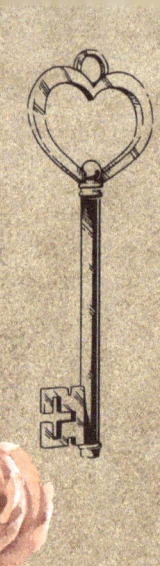

**IF ONLY I COULD HOLD ON TO WHAT IT ONCE FELT TO BE HUMAN,**

Maybe then I wouldn't have
grown so distant from
the life I have been given
Numbness into numbness
I am slowly sinking under,
I think these bones have
found my grave before my
heart is ready for its final stage

When I close my eyes I can see
the place where I once knew
what it meant to feel alive,
It's like a shadow
hanging over me,
but not entirely all of me
I know this place still exists
and it's me who has changed
If only I can hold on to
what it means to feel human

*Denae Terese Hintze*

Depression happens when
your mind doesn't find
fulfillment in the work
you put into

Some spend their entire lives
believing money
equals happiness,

but they forget
happiness is wholeness

The past, present, and future all live precariously through these same four walls. I lie in this room imagining all the moments that have weaved in and out between them. Similar to the walls of my mind from when I first saw daylight. When I first saw the same streets, trees, and hilltops meeting our every sunrise and sunset through the horizon with each repeating day.

I stop and look up at the ceiling but take myself out, as if these walls can also be shaped by perception. A story to tell of a past connected to a future that hasn't lost its touch yet. This is the stillness that consumes me, that I find myself escaping to. This is the very space I believe is where our future lies.

If just for a moment everything is alright.

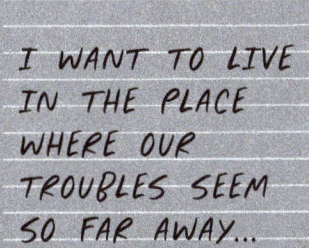

I WANT TO LIVE IN THE PLACE WHERE OUR TROUBLES SEEM SO FAR AWAY...

### Sunday afternoon ✾

Sometimes I fall silent. Sometimes interacting with the world becomes difficult. I am finding I escape myself to come back to myself.. I mean, we are the creators of our world, right? I believe it was Jim Carrey that once said, "Depression is your avatar telling you it's tired of being the character you're trying to play," and that resonates with me deeply.. I think we as humans are meant to grow as naturally as a tree in the breeze, or the way the waves meet the shore, a flower in bloom. Instead, we find ourselves being brought into these intricate lives, sacrificing our chance to bloom in the process of fighting for survival.

I don't have answers for everything, but what I do consider is that maybe we are on the verge of something more, something greater.. & we're just caught up. Maybe we have an idea of what productivity means, but sometimes I think we fool ourselves into aligning that with the forces at hand rather than living through our hearts. I feel productivity should resonate with our sense of being that encourages homeostasis. Not just fulfilling obligations and treating them as the only accomplishments we deserve (for some, this might be enough.. but not for everyone).

It's no wonder why there are those who hit a certain age, question their lives and call it a "mid-life crisis". It's crap. "Mid-life crisis" means your life got away from you with the time you already had, and you wonder where it went because you forgot you had a say in it, too.

So while I am caught up in my own life, sometimes I fall silent and interacting becomes difficult. The silence can be relieving but almost addicting. I have to push myself to continue on, or embrace a moment that will allow me to feel more authentic. Maybe these little pushes will create a bigger change in the grand scheme of things. I worry though there will come a day where I won't have strength left in my fight. Before that time comes, I hope to find a place where I won't have to escape myself ever again.

A METAMORPHIC ACCIDENT

We cling to a story
older than our existence
Brought into a past
with no future to rely on
Taking shape to the roles
we've built dependence on
Validating our existence
by our successes, and rarely
what we hold inside

Looking too closely with
our lens out of focus,
There is more to this story,
a truth beyond our senses
May there come a day we
won't have to fall back in line,
Where the soul of the world
and human nature align

UNDER FOG-FILLED SKIES, THIS PLACE
CAN SURE FEEL HOLLOW SOMETIMES
MY HEART IS LOST DEEP
IN THE FOREST, LUNGS DETACHED
FROM MY BODY,

I can be found somewhere between what you see and how I think, dissociation comes from my recognition of a manufactured reality. At times I feel claustrophobic in all of this mobility, like there is someting more I know I can feel. I am an illiterate to a future society, aching to redefine our evolutive casualty. A heart beating in philanthropy.

HOW LAND MEETS SALT DISSOLVING TO SEA

WE'LL LIGHT CANDLES TO KEEP THE FIRE BURNING INSIDE OUR HEARTS AND MINDS,

Denae Terese Hintze

SEEK CONNECTION IN
DROUGHTS AND LOST DIRECTION,
FINDING A THREAD TO
HOLD ON TO WORTHWHILE

We are the voice of those
who have been forgotten,
Souls that lived before us
though their bodies have befallen
We have been given new air to breathe,
but feel the echoes of their needs

Why does it feel like we
are always on borrowed time?
Is it because of the lives we
live that we still have yet to define?
Twenty-four hours
in a day never seems like enough,
Sacrificing who we are,
falling into the daily rush

There is beauty here to attain
in all that remains,
Our lungs are still breathing
every day a chance to give new meaning
Clinch the more to life
outside our daily strife,
Give peace to those at rest
knowing that we tried our best,
Remember we are nature in skin
There is a wild that deserves to be lived

TO FIND STRENGTH IN
A SECOND WAVE OF LIFE

I WONDER WHO I WOULD BE TODAY
 IF I HADN'T SPENT ALL OF MY
YESTERDAY'S CHASING AFTER
THE WRONG THINGS

OR MAYBE ALL THE THINGS
 I HAVE BEEN DRAWN TO UP UNTIL NOW
ARE SUPPOSED TO LEAD ME TO
  WHO I AM MEANT TO BECOME

I WAS MADE FOR MOVING,
 MY LIFE IN MID-AIR
  LITERALLY AND METAPHORICALLY,
 ATOMS CONNECTED BY HEARTSTRINGS,
  NEVER INTENDED TO STAY IN ONE PLACE

Letters From Gardenia

Waking up to my own rhythm

The taste of the first cup of coffee

Quiet mornings with the sound
of birds outside my window

Smell of fresh air

What moments feel like without time

Writing a steady flow of how I feel inside

The sight of an ocean, mountain, or forest

As well as the hustle of a city
and people watching

Learning what others are like

Laughing until my lungs collapse

Spontaneous moments with those I love

Campfires under countless stars

Being surrounded by lightning bugs

Finding music that understands me

The feeling you get right before you
fall asleep and your eyes become heavy

> I wonder what we
> were like from
> the very beginning,
> Before the Earth placed
> its mark on us
> the mind untouched
> in its purest form
> What was the tone
> of our thoughts?

**HOW DIFFERENT WOULD WE BE IF WE TRULY LET OUR SOULS BREATHE?**

*Denae Terese Hintze*

These are the same two eyes
that first saw daylight,
I can only imagine
what I dreamt of in the
womb under our moonlight

Mother's silent whispers of
'I love you' gave promise
of a peaceful place,
As do the trees
swaying in the breeze,
giving each breath
our saving grace

If only we remembered the
way the world used to seem,
Maybe then would we be
gifted new eyes to see

I want to see us stripped
Stripped of how we once felt,
and how we have come to see
Stripped of opinions of ourselves,
and how relationships can be
Allowing us to view
the world in new ways,
Recognizing truths hidden
amongst our every day
Hearing echoes of antiquity,
of all the words
that were left behind,
Connecting our past to the future,
History to the undefinable,
Realizing we are the
tangible in between,
The power to create
a life of our dreams

WHEN OUR FACTS OF LIFE
   HAVE BEEN ALL SORTED OUT
   AND OUR TIMING FALL INTO PLACE,
   IT IS THEN WHEN OUR
   HERAT SPACE WILL FIND
      ITS STRENGTH

TIME TOLD ME OLD LEAVES
MUST ABIDE BY MEMORY,
BUT STARS SHINE
TO REMIND ME NOT
EVERYTHING IS AS IT SEEMS

A PLACE WHERE HUMAN AND NATURE ALIGN,

HEART MEETS MIND,

**WEDNESDAY**

I have this theory that our souls
breathe life into this matter,
while matter solidifies our existence.
We are born into the all unknowingness,
our soul latches on to our mind's
appeal at almost everything we come
into contact with.
Over time, we become used to this matter
making life more complex in an attempt
to live in synchronicity.

Some might say to overcome this other-worldly anxiety is to accept what is and let go of what we cannot control. Well I say it is bullshit, I think it's something we tell ourselves to do away with the facts of life. In realisation that our lives are not entirely our own, we are always at partial sacrifice of where we stand as a species.

I believe my longing for the other-world is not something to tame, but it is a natural way of life that I hope someday humanity can embody completely. I have these moments where my soul and matter are aligned, a temporary elation in a moment or freedom of thought that I end up having to walk away from and cover up again. Cage my essence and brave the weather... How can life be such a beautiful, tragic thing?

Denae Terese Hintze

THE SOUND OF
GHOSTS RANG
IN UNISON, DEAD
POETS HAUNTING
BENEATH THE TREES

SOMETIMES I
WONDER IF OUR
HEARTS ONCE
BEAT THE SAME,
ACHING FOR
FREEDOM BEFORE
OUR FINAL
REST IN PEACE

In my opinion the government is like a double-edged sword. In a lot of cases they are here to protect our people and our rights, what often goes unnoticed though are the things we don't want to believe to be true. That power can dictate our freedom.

I am someone who feels oppression no matter what surface matters are being heavily orchestrated. Mine is underneath, the hidden reality of our times. How I once thought life to be magic, but rather a false flame in a world of make believe, except this isn't a fairytale.. It's more of a martyr-tale.

[I BELIEVE THERE IS ROOM TO REDEFINE WHAT IT MEANS TO BE FREE]

Denae Terese Hintze

These two feet share the same grounds as you,
even if from across the globe

Our hearts with different beats
all drumming to the same song

Somewhere we will find peace
Somewhere we will find unison

105

With an acquired awareness
of all things connected,
I am more than just
a single perspective
May it be the sunlight
peeking through
every morning dew,
A symphony of nature
rising into every day anew

There is a truth to be
found in every
moment passing,
An eternal message
to learn from
every disaster
May we find strength
in our hearts no matter
how far we wander,
Find nature to be
a commonplace,
in every
birthright to honor

What if we saw this as a blank canvas rather than our inheritance, Practiced restoration despite our indifferences, Found mutual ground to turn this world around, and remember our place here is impermanent We could build a future where nature meets human, Allow our common ground to grow into a union, One we are proud of the inheritance we are giving, Revive our planet, returning to its natural rhythm

This moment is all I ever have,
Everything else that passed
is just a memory
It comes from my left, right brain
It doesn't have to affect here and now
this moment is all I ever have,
I need to stop chasing thoughts
that fill the emptiness of this room,
and hold on to this moment
as if this room is all I ever knew

Have you ever wondered
what it is like for others
to see you for the first time?

I am not sure if there are words
to put into the emotions I have
once felt seeing another
for the first time,
I just wish I could have
shared it with them

A color only I know
and reaction to how intense
their presence can affect
others around them


I think we forget we are magic

*Denae Terese Hintze*

Memory

Some distant twitch interfering
the present, a repeat of moments
from only your point of view,
destined to make you believe
that it was better
than here and now,
leaving a melancholy emptiness
at the pit of your stomach
as if joy can never be found again

[But it can]

*Letters From Gardenia*

ART IS THE INSPIRATION

BORN FROM OUR OBJECTIVE

# LIFE, A CONSTANT MOTION TO SEE, FEEL, AND THINK

How ironic it is to be a mortal composition
The art of life though a temporal disposition,
Our desire to remain beating should be more than just a physical evolution

# Sketchbook mockup

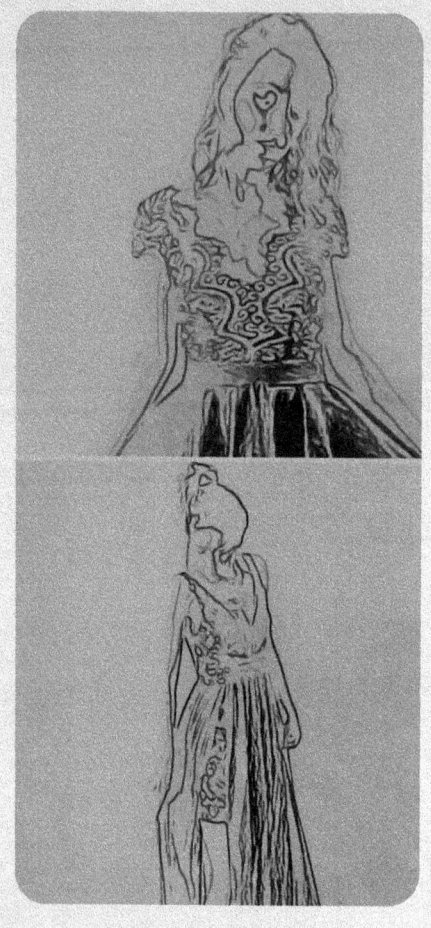

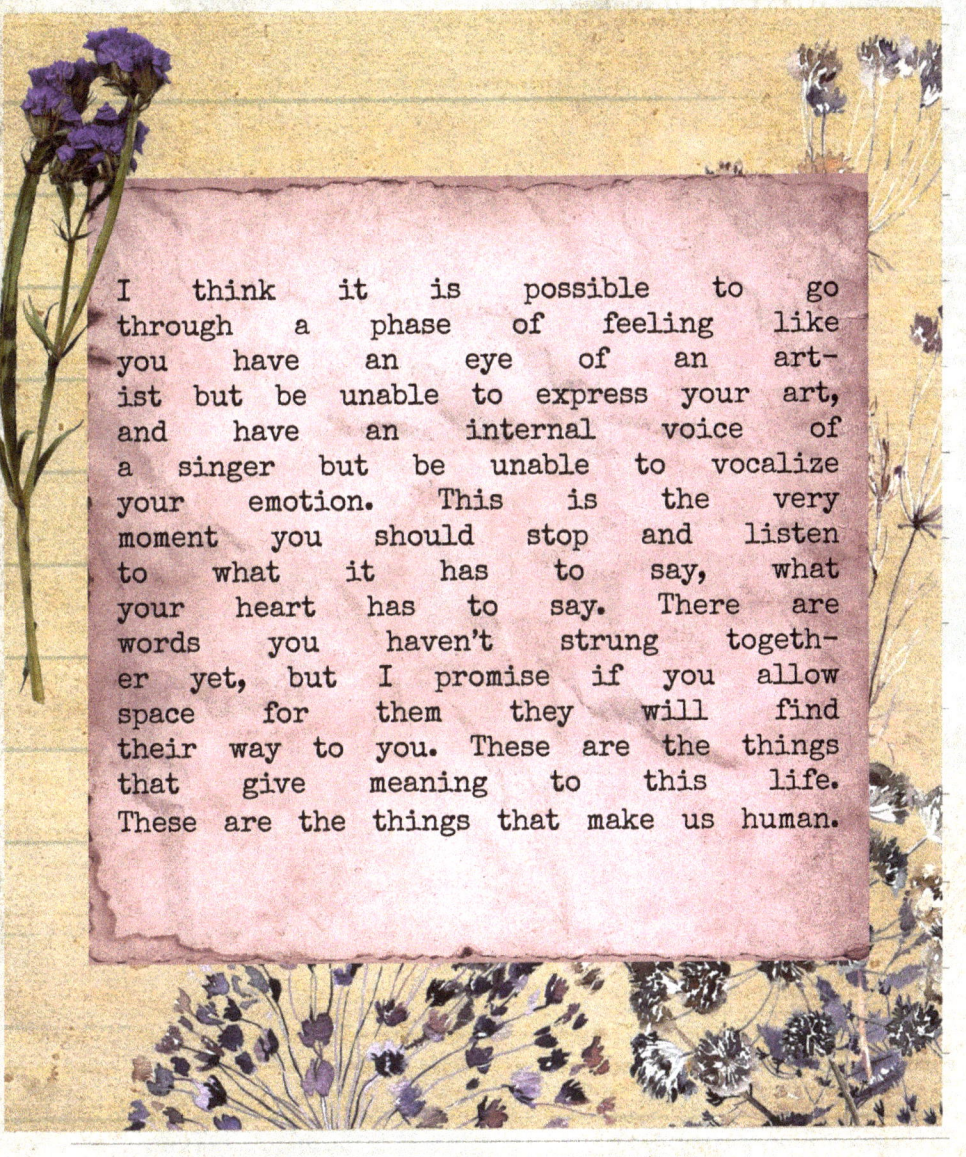

I think it is possible to go through a phase of feeling like you have an eye of an artist but be unable to express your art, and have an internal voice of a singer but be unable to vocalize your emotion. This is the very moment you should stop and listen to what it has to say, what your heart has to say. There are words you haven't strung together yet, but I promise if you allow space for them they will find their way to you. These are the things that give meaning to this life. These are the things that make us human.

*Letters From Gardenia*

FIND

THE SPACE

INSIDE

YOUR

THOUGHTS

where judgement
can be forgotten,
A place where all the noise
and afterthoughts
set into the horizon
There is clarity to be found
in this momentary stillness,
Space for new air to breathe,
A mind without resistance

ST. THOMAS
U.S. VIRGIN ISLANDS
2017

The hardest mornings are the ones where you can still taste the night before on your lips, hungover and moving in slow motion. I remember my feet felt like they were moving through molasses, but I was on vacation and no amount of dehydration could have ruined the tone of the day for me. We made it to a small cafe down in Charlotte Amalie. It was at that moment I really felt the essence of the island, or what some might call energy. Whether or not you believe, what I feel is always real to me.

Stepping foot at the breakfast bar, I sat next to a gentleman reading a newspaper. I looked around at the pace of everything, moving ever so naturally. No bothersome technology or the rush of daily life, no floating thoughts. The employees somehow even felt at ease. The door was open to fresh air and sunlight, which made everything feel that much more alive. All of us just

existing in the moment, experiencing it for what it was. No matter how insignificant that might have been, I will always look back at that yellow cafe and think of it fondly. The way life could be.

Denae Terese Hintze

I WANT TO LIVE IN THE PLACES WHERE

THE PEOPLE NEVER STOP GROWING

*Letters From Gardenia*

If we are made of star stuff
created billions of years ago,
that means that is how long
it took for us to come into
consciousness of a single
moment in time that might
feel ordinary to us,
but rather it is
extraordinary
to be moving
in all this star stuff

I am the secrets
of the wind,
A storm of energy
dancing from within,
trying to express
a way to be found

THE SMELL OF CAMPFIRES
IN A WARM SUMMER BREEZE

REMIND ME OF
CHILDHOOD AND FREEDOM

Back to times of walking barefoot and hayrides, dancing and losing all sense of time

This is the place my family goes to escape, I now know this is the place my family goes to come back to themselves

To remind them of who they are outside of everyday lives

WHY DOES EVERYTHING FEEL SMALLER

THAN WHEN I WAS A CHILD?

THERE SHOULD BE NO LIMITS

WHEN MASTERING THE WILD

Some might feel our nature dissipates with age, though a part of me believes it begins to fade the more time we spend away

Our thoughts grow louder as our senses become softer, leaving us empty of the thing that brings life to this matter I know creation still exists all around us and it's our reality that can be deceiving

Our world can grow again as long as we give our nature new meaning

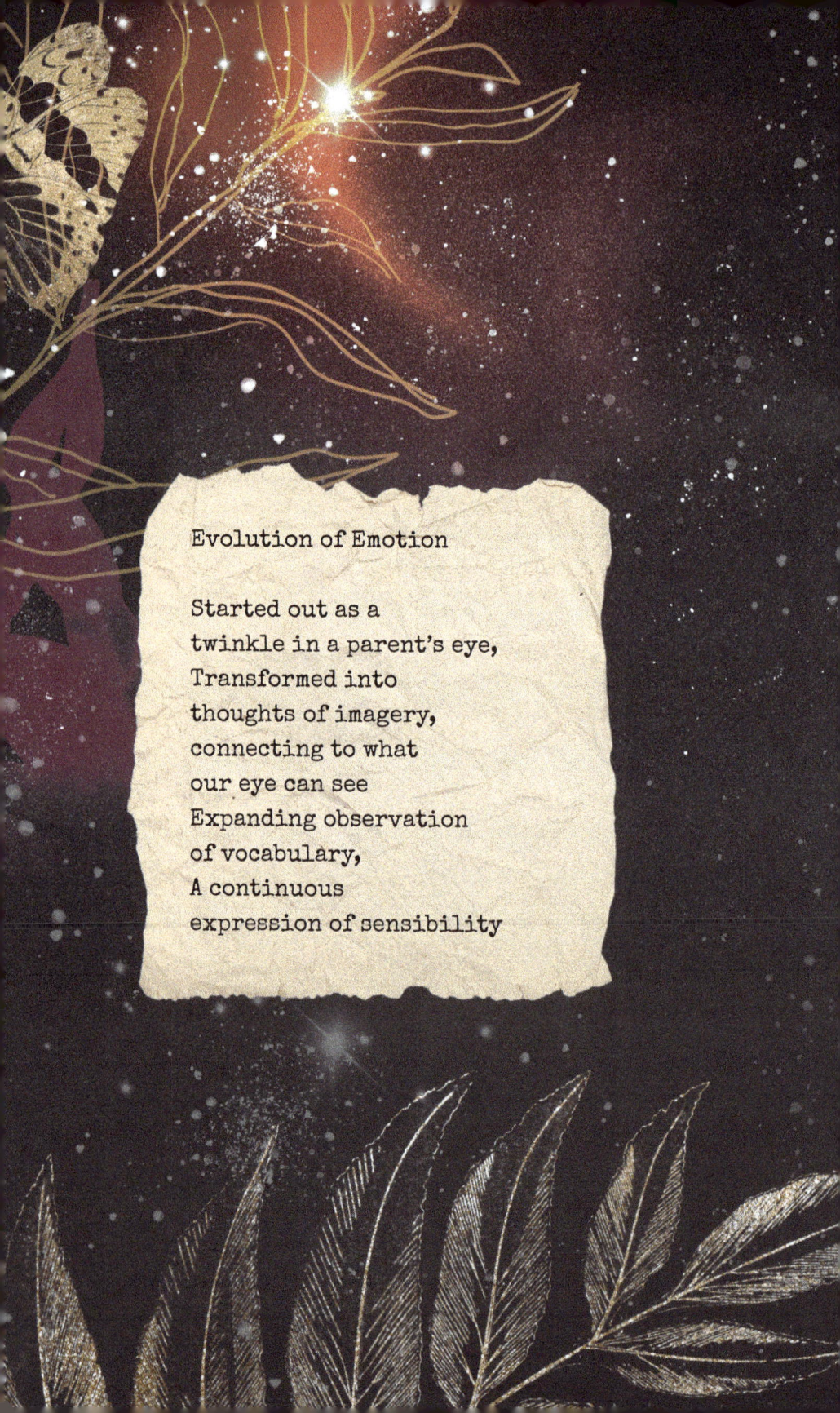

Evolution of Emotion

Started out as a
twinkle in a parent's eye,
Transformed into
thoughts of imagery,
connecting to what
our eye can see
Expanding observation
of vocabulary,
A continuous
expression of sensibility

**Consciousness**

If everything
has consciousness,
how does the Moon
feel about the sky?
How does the Sun
look me in the eye?

Sunrise to sunset, sunrise to sunset
Our dying star a reminder of all
the land I haven't met yet
Her and I are much the same,
our depth shines bright
despite our mortal fate

Is it ironic her warmth is
our Earth's compatibility?
We are a life expression of our
Sun's reflection in soul familiarity

My beating heart lies awake at night
longing to redefine what
my own life means,
Starry nights
blending into daydreams
of distant lands
connecting sea to sea

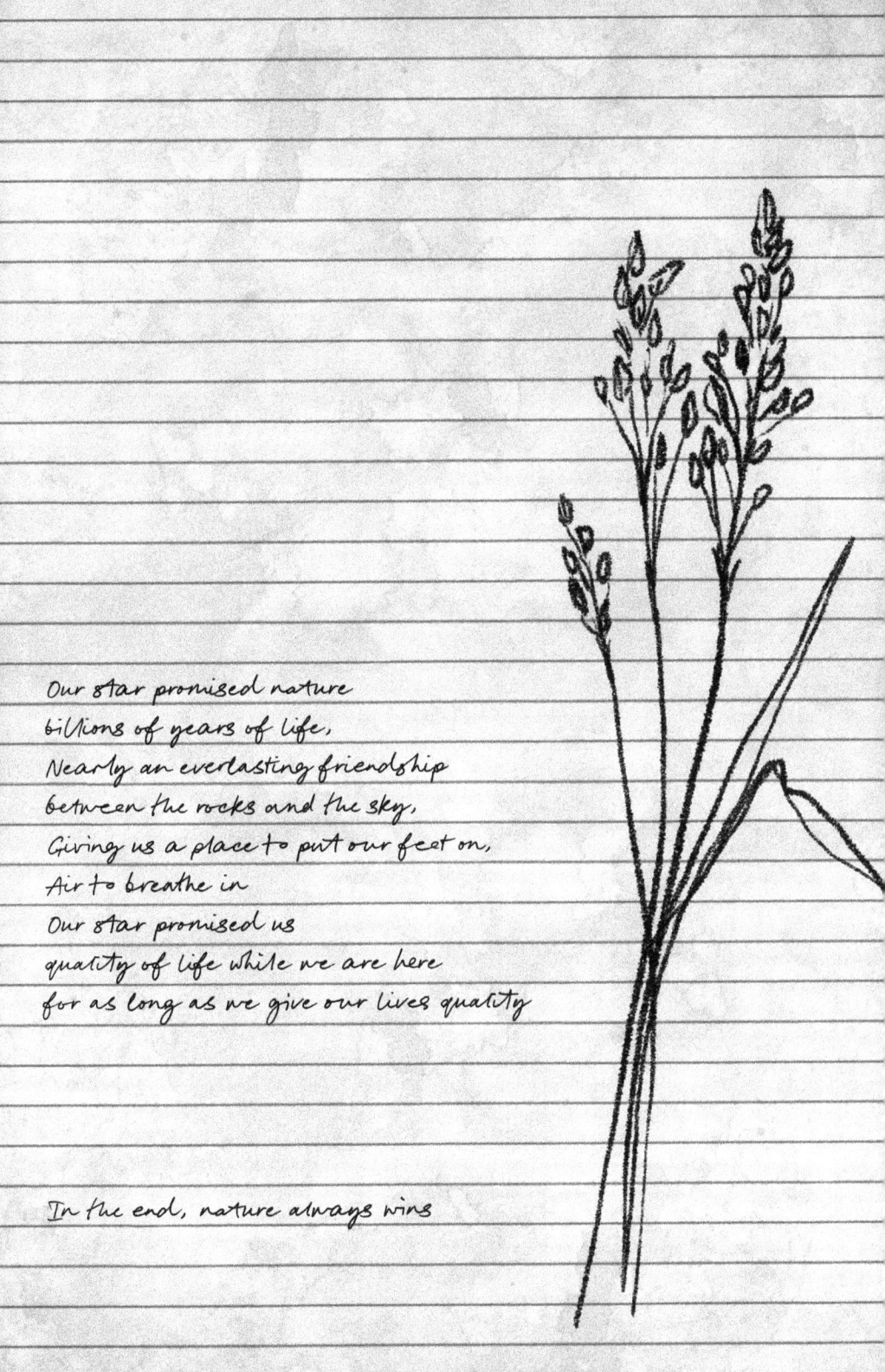

Our star promised nature
billions of years of life,
Nearly an everlasting friendship
between the rocks and the sky,
Giving us a place to put our feet on,
Air to breathe in
Our star promised us
quality of life while we are here
for as long as we give our lives quality

In the end, nature always wins

IF WE EXPERIENCED A MODERN
CREATIVE EXPLOSION
SOME 40,000 YEARS AGO,
I HAVE EVERY REASON TO BELIEVE
THAT IT CAN HAPPEN AGAIN
THAT WE CAN SAVE OURSELVES
FROM THE REALITY WE ENDURE... AGAIN

It's year 2989

1,000 years after I was born

Just eleven years shy of the great 3000
I still remember the Y2K and end of all times,
Fear of technological disruption,
"The Last Days" according to religion,
and any other confusion
we tirelessly imposed on ourselves

We had a way of doing that.
Because of how far
our hearts were from our minds,
it was almost like a psychosis
subconsciously took over,
The circus could have went on forever

But there was a fallout between our
masquerade and the self-proclaimed,
Manipulation became harder to attain
Whoever we were, our hearts
began to beat louder
There was no avoiding it,
The waves took a hit on
every personal embodiment

Wherever we were, the beating
brought our minds into focus,
What used to make sense
started to feel irrelevant
Our hearts at play
in a state of discontent
Remembering life before
constraint, demand, or disconnect


Remembering our humanity
despite our deeper intellect

As the dust settles
and all of us become
ancient history,
I hope someone
in the far future
reflects back at us
as the recognition
of a sacrifice,

A seed to another story
of where it all began

Letters From Gardenia

OUR LIVES
ARE AN EXTENSION
FROM THE FIRST DAY
WE WERE BORN

Sometimes I get this feeling like it is almost hard to believe that this is the same life I was brought up in. That I have made it this far, this long. If only humans could retain the memory of every single thing we've ever been through, how different our lives would be today. How much more conscious we would be in every passing moment, rather than being just a reflection of the events that happened to us. I am always feeling like I am a glimpse of my entirety, never feeling completely all of me. Always in transition, but also recognizing how beautiful it can be at the same time.

My grandma always tells me a story about her mother. How she used to tell her life is like watching a movie and then it's over. I wonder what that means to her, how she considers that when thinking back on her own life.

As for my own I know that with every passing breath, every heartbeat, no matter how mundane,

I'm alive. I'm alive. I'm alive. ♡

*Letters From Gardenia*

I WANT TO WAKE UP
 IN DIFFERENT CITIES,
NEVER MISS A SUNRISE OR SUNSET,
REMEMBER TO LOOK AT THE STARS
 MORE THAN TIME ITSELF
   EMBRACE THE FEELING OF BEING HUMAN,
    FOR IT IS MY ANCESTORS CALL OF THE WILD
   STEMMING FROM WHEN THEY WERE A CHILD

The silence into
the night,
A lonesome
crept in feeling
that gives weakness
to my strength of five

Realizing our empty existence
in the vastness of the sky,
How small I feel yet
expansive at the same time
To have a heart
in a home of wandering eyes

Denae Terese Hintze

*Letters From Gardenia*

Sun kissed by starlight,
our lives have
surely been defined
From dust to return to dust,
we are the star-seeds
coincidentally aligned

Denae Terese Hintze

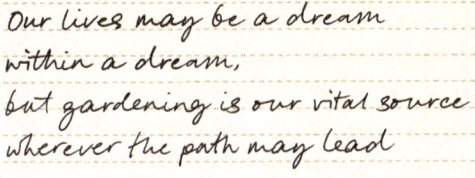

Our lives may be a dream
within a dream,
but gardening is our vital source
wherever the path may lead

Letters From Gardenia

> BEFORE LANGUAGE, PEOPLE WOULD
> FALL IN LOVE JUST BY
> THE PRESENCE OF ANOTHER,
> THE ART OF SILENT INTERACTION

### Denae Terese Hintze

Your essence is illuminating, can you feel mine too?

**Wednesday Afternoon**

I am thirty-two years and have yet to come in contact with a living and breathing version of an honest, romantic love. The only thing my past has taught me is not everything is as it seems. I can't tell you how many times I have fallen into moments of trickery and feeling like I was truly being seen. I remind myself though that just because I have yet to encounter a soul-mate, doesn't mean they are inexistent. While I am lost, I am also in the midst of all the love that surrounds me, and maybe just not a part of me. Today I dedicate myself to embracing what that love means for me, and imagine what it would be like if I were to ever experience it for myself.

*The following page is a story of a boy I never met.*

Today began like any other day for me, until I found a broad distinction between the time before I met him and the time after. These moments come to us like magic, wake us up from our sleep and remind us of why we are still alive.
Anyone who does not believe in love at first sight has never locked eyes with someone they had never met, and felt the energy of the Universe dancing within a single glance.

A sudden familiarity washed over me, as if he was someone I was searching for all along. The way he spoke to me was like music, I don't think I could ever get tired of listening to him express his world. He was beautiful for the way he carried himself, and when he looked at me I finally knew what it felt like to be found. There was no pretense or complexities, we just were.

We both knew there was a life before and a life after the moment we locked eyes.

Innocence is a fire within us,
it never really burns out
Its embers keep us warm
if we were ever to be lead astray
Desire, often overthrown by shame
as our morals prod at us
while feeding into our
human essence

Hearticulation, a defining factor
Some may be out of touch,
mastering only the surface
of what we are truly after

For mind and heart
go hand in hand,
with one we could be
lost without the other.
Subconsciously seeking meaning,
oblivious of our resistance,
what may be quiet could
remain beating.

You and I appear the same.
Though from embers to flame,
it's hard to read between the lines
Just two souls crossing paths
on a vague foundation,
How does one avoid the shallows
in search of more of
what our hearts can truly define?

I know physical touch can be
an immediate temptation,
 For everyone it's different,
but there is only one magnetic attraction
  Some might scratch the surface
while others feel it deeper,
  Though it's mostly just a chemical reaction
as each body gets closer

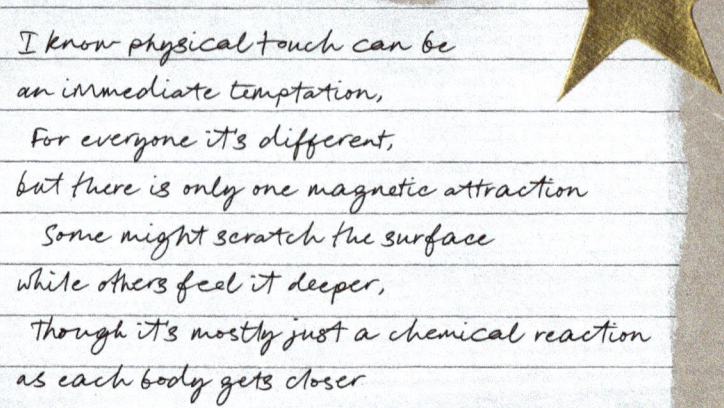

There is one painful thing
 I can see in sight,
is the one whose heart is sinking
  into a story as old as time
   It's a simple misinterpretation
   of an intimate reaction,
   two hearts on separate journeys
    who failed to read
    between the lines

Denae Terese Hintze

Do you ever wonder
why our generation
is full of disfigured hearts?
Maybe it's false intention
that leads to disillusion
from the start
There is one solution
that comes to mind
when chaos become too confined
Is to never give up
on what you believe,
but don't always
trust everything you see
Hope someday someone
will meet you where you are,
and all that fog of broken lust
will become a memory
fading into the stars

IF YOU EVER FIND SOMEONE
WHO LOVES YOU THE WAY YOU HOPED,
BUT THOSE FEELINGS
ARE NOT BEING RECIPROCATED
I HOPE YOU HAVE ENOUGH RESPECT
FOR THEM TO SET THEM FREE

(Everyone deserves the love they long for)

At the end of the phone
full of empty responses,
my heart stuck in place
while my mind
tells me to walk away

I am realizing
one of the most bravest
things someone can do
is let go of what
they thought to be true

Trading disillusion
for the possibility of
someone who actually
beats for you

HE WAS A STORM CHASING THE NIGHT
LOST BETWEEN DANCES

A GUARDED HEART WHO
FAILED TO SEE WHERE
TRUE ROMANCE LIES

His storm of the night was similar to my own,

Except I left my heart wide open I was chasing the dance getting lost in false romance

*Letters From Gardenia*

I AM A VICTIM OF FALLING IN LOVE AT FIRST SIGHT THOSE WHO HAVE EXPERIENCED IT SECONDHAND MAY NOT HAVE BELIEVED IN MY INTENSITY, BUT MY HEART ALWAYS HAD THE BEST OF ME

Do you think our hearts
break more over the idea
of how we encounter another?

Our paths may intersect,
but you may never
see what I see,
even if you were there
to see it too

How can perspective
be our greatest divide,
but strongest when
intertwined, if by chance
two souls are able
to see eye to eye?

A THOUSAND LOVES ALWAYS SHIFTING
INTO THE DEPTHS OF TOMORROW

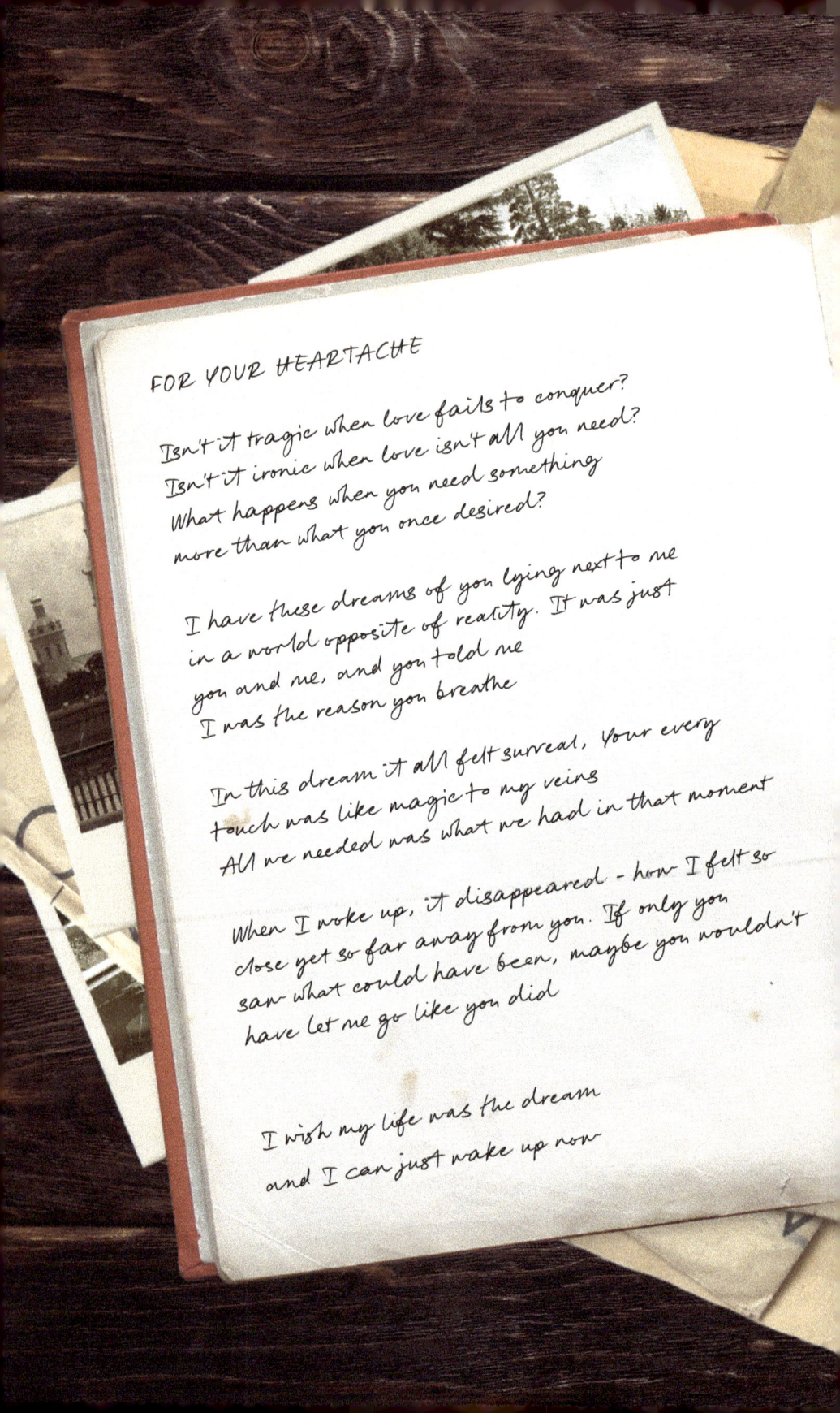

# FOR YOUR HEARTACHE

Isn't it tragic when love fails to conquer?
Isn't it ironic when love isn't all you need?
What happens when you need something
more than what you once desired?

I have these dreams of you lying next to me
in a world opposite of reality. It was just
you and me, and you told me
I was the reason you breathe

In this dream it all felt surreal, Your every
touch was like magic to my veins
All we needed was what we had in that moment

When I woke up, it disappeared - how I felt so
close yet so far away from you. If only you
saw what could have been, maybe you wouldn't
have let me go like you did

I wish my life was the dream
and I can just wake up now

Sorrow

These eyes are not made to see
a brighter day from shades of grey
Sorrow is the one thing I cannot handle
It is the morning light
peeking through my bedroom window
It is the every move I take on in a day
It is the damage between you and me
It is the one more drink until I go sleep
Every inch, every word
sorrow will soak through into another world
There is no way of stopping it,
no way of escaping it
Just when I think sorrow is over,
Its shadow follows me
and eventually becomes a part of me
Sorrow is the message I send to you,
It is the one more day not near you
It is the emptiness in my heart,
and the tear in my eye
when I have to tell you goodbye
I know I can't fight it,
and I cannot hide it
Until something better comes my way,
then it will just naturally fade away

SHE IS A BEAUTIFUL CONTRADICTION,
FILLS HER HEAD
OF LOVE WITHOUT CONVICTION,
DAYDREAMS OF LOVE
    WITHOUT CONDITION,
BUT WILL LOOK PAST
    EVERYONE IN HER DIRECTION

I fear I will
spend my whole life
waiting for an idea
of what love can be,
Never finding someone
who sees me for me,
It's like I can feel it from
within yearning to be let out,
Chasing after a reflection
of the love I already have,
Feeling incomplete until
I am able to find it
in someone else,
If I can just accept
its worth within myself,
Only then will I realize
I never needed to be seen,
but rather longed to be seen
in the eyes of someone
other than me

TODAY I AM ACTIVELY CHOOSING
TO LET GO OF THE UNREQUITED
WEIGHING ME DOWN

INSTEAD, I WILL LEARN TO GROW
IN THE SPACES OF MY OWN HEART

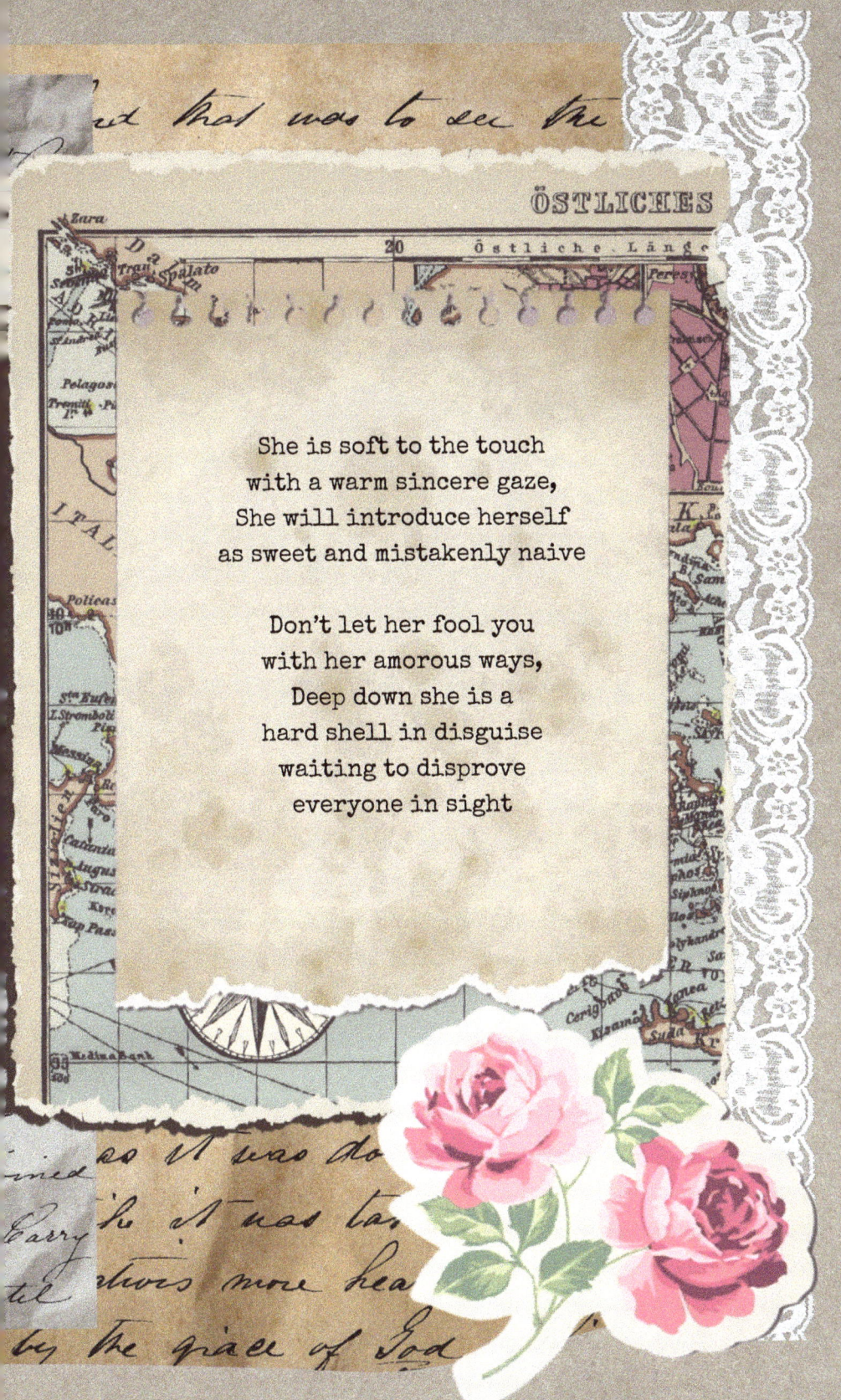

She is soft to the touch
with a warm sincere gaze,
She will introduce herself
as sweet and mistakenly naive

Don't let her fool you
with her amorous ways,
Deep down she is a
hard shell in disguise
waiting to disprove
everyone in sight

Denae Terese Hintze

I think of my experiences
tracing down to the lovers
that passed me by,
I can't help but think
how they did me a favor
because of all the growth
I see in myself now
that their time has passed

Yes I may be rough
around the edges,
But there are also parts
of me I love that maybe
wouldn't exist without
having known them

So for all of the heartaches
you put me through,
I forgive you

## TUESDAY EVENING

I find myself in art and lyrics,
experiences and places that resonate with me
even long after I have left them behind
I find myself in chance encounters,
in people I wish I could
meet again for the first time
In all the moments that lead to now,
I am left here with questions in my mind,
Will I wander my whole life?
Will I continue to sacrifice
complacency for the possibility
of redefining what love truly means?

Have I ever found what love truly means?

I search for worlds mind after mind,
Only ever reaching the surface of what's inside
Maybe I am doing this wrong, I tell myself
Or maybe there is more I haven't discovered yet
In another with a depth I haven't met yet,
but the questions at hand still remain

Will I wander my whole life?
Will I ever be able to find a place
where complacency meets complexity
in someone who sees eye to eye with me?
For the possibility of a deeper soul compatibility

live in the moment,
let go of thoughts
and strengthen my senses,
listen to the soft sounds
of birds outside my window
with the smell of fresh air,
Make more room for
Innocent space again

Denae Terese Hintze

I BELIEVE

   THE PERMANENCE OF

      OUR IMPERMANENCE IS LOVE

Dear Reader,

If you found this book in your hands, you have helped me more than you know and I can only hope these words do the same for you. Thank you for seeing something in me worth holding onto, a gaze into my inner world that desires to be heard. Words are magic to our soul, breath to our lungs, and key to connection with this world and everyone around us. I feel it is important to remain soulful outside of our daily tasks, outside of living life so faintly. There are ways of keeping our spark alive despite our circumstances if we take the time to seek it.

I hope you always find yourself in places where the people never stop growing <3

Love, Denae

Acknowledgements

When I consider those I am thankful for, I would say just about anyone I have crossed paths with in my lifetime. Whether we are family, friends or foes, a stranger passerby, all of you helped shape me in some way into who I am meant to become.

A butterfly effect of random happenings
which is still happening, so thank you.

I especially thank my mother, Del Mar Rita, and father, Brian Hintze, for always being there for me with unconditional love. I am not sure I would be as strong as I am today without your support. You guys are the most sincere and bravest people I know that would do anything for those they love.

My dad is no longer with us, but I know he would want to see me shine. When asking who I wanted to be when I grew up as a child, he would always say to me, "I can see you being a star, singing the national anthem at football games like those girls you see on TV," and this is sort of that moment for me, but in a more subtle way. I hope in my heart of hearts he is somehow here to see this.

## Acknowledgements Cont'd

I also want to thank my brother, Jeff Hintze, who always looked out for me and has been there since day one. The rest of my immediate family members who want nothing but the best for us.

From Calina Rita-Cina, Brenda Hintze-O'brien and Joe O'brien, Mary Brunner-Hintze and Robert Hintze, Ellen Daley-Schulz and Steve Schulz, Ramona Rita and Les Turbat, and all of my grandparents and cousins. Barbara Hintze and Robert Hintze, Theresa Rita and Robert Rita, Cassandra Cina-Munoz, Esme Lucas, Sam Cina, Matt Cina.

You are all amazing, I love you!

## About the Poet

Like many of us, Denae was born made for dreams to help shape this world. Striving through transformation and adaptivity, she became drawn to the healing of words and magic of imagination. Where creativity meets truth, Denae finds herself on a journey of looking inward to a world unbeknownst to the rest. From the moment she met herself at this level, she became overwhelmed by the sensation of wanting to touch the lives of others. She sees potential that shines brighter than the defaults of this reality, and spends her time trying to become how it makes her feel. Seeking solace in her writing, here is a woman who chooses herself every day despite the circumstances surrounding us. Here is a woman who believes in a future where we are all more connected, not only to each other but with the very grounds we walk on, Mother Nature.

Don't ever let anyone
steal your light away.
Always remember
to love deeply,
and bring color
to everyone's life.

FOLLOW MY JOURNEY
@D.TERESE_
ON INSTAGRAM

Copyright © 2022 by Denae Terese Hintze.
ALL RIGHTS RESERVED.
NO PART OF THIS BOOK MAY BE USED
OR REPRODUCED WITHOUT WRITTEN PERMISSION
FROM THE AUTHOR


Words and design by Denae Terese Hintze.
Cover photo by Denae Terese Hintze.
Inside photography by Denae Terese Hintze.
Black and white illustrations drawn by Del Mar T. Rita.
Home floor plans designed by Brian Jeff Hintze.
Watercolor paintings by Vera Gorbunova.
Digital clipart by various artists found on Etsy,
Canva, Pixabay, Unsplash, and Rawpixel.

Photographs featured in this book were taken by
Denae Terese in Illinois, Colorado, North Carolina,
Tennesse, St. Thomas U.S. Virgin Islands, Mexico,
Florida, and Michigan. Particular places she stayed at
include Art Farm Fennville, Prince Bay Farm,
and Borrowed Time.